Keto Fat Bombs: 30 Chocolate Fat Bomb Recipes and Keto Fat Bombs Snacks

Energy Boosting Choco Keto Fat Bombs Cookbook with Easy to Make Sweet Chocolate Fat Bomb Cookies and Sugar Free Keto Desserts

By Brendan Fawn

Table of Contents

Legal & Disclaimer

Introduction

This cookbook contains delicious and tasty chocolate ketogenic fat bomb desserts that are low in carb, but high in fat and contain mainly natural sweeteners such as stevia, monk fruit sweetener or others. The main reason why chocolate keto fat bombs are the best solution for you if you want to eat something sweet, but still healthy is that there is no need to deprive yourself of delicious sweet things if your goal is to lose weight, belly or hips fat, stay in shape or simply maintain the good condition of your body.

Chocolate is crucial for our health, because it contains a lot of different vitamins. Many people that use a ketogenic diet include chocolate keto fat bombs as a part of their fat bombs or keto diets because chocolate keto bombs are very simple and fast to prepare and contain a lot of vital elements and minerals.

Enjoy a collection of 30 mouthwatering chocolate keto fat bomb recipes from this cookbook while you work towards your health goals or just want to eat healthy sweets.

Truly Yours,

Brendan Fawn

About the Chocolate Keto Fat Bombs
What are the Chocolate Keto Fat Bombs?

There are different chocolate types and tastes, which contain vitamins that are important to our bodies, such as vitamin A, E, K, Thiamine B1, Riboflavin B2, B3, B6, B12 and much more. That is why chocolate keto fat bombs are healthy and crucial in your keto diet. Moreover, choco fat bombs have low and medium amounts of proteins, low amounts of carbs, but a high content of fats. Chocolate keto fat bombs contain such fats as chocolate butter, cocoa butter, cocoa powder, coconut butter or coconut oil.

Chocolate fat bombs are small snacks that make an excellent source of energy for those who are on a low-carb diet and want to eat something sweet but with a high level of healthy fats. Choco keto fat bombs don't contain unhealthy sugars. Instead, the keto chocolate bombs contain various sweeteners −monk fruit, stevia, xylitol and others.

The main advantage of the chocolate fat bombs is that they contain simple ingredients that you can buy online or in every corner shop and can be prepared very fast. Cocoa powder or dark chocolate are the ingredients that could be found simply everywhere. Moreover, it is easy to maintain control over the nutrients and sweet bombs portions you eat every day. If you are busy during the day, and you don't have time to prepare something healthy and sweet for yourself, but you want to eat healthy sweet things and follow the ketogenic path at the same time, then the chocolate keto fat bombs would be an ideal solution for you!

Main Characteristics of the Chocolate Keto Fat Bombs

- Contain unsweetened dark, white or milk chocolate, cocoa powder, unsweetened chocolate butter, sugar-free hazelnut chocolate spread, cocoa butter

- Contain low carb, high healthy fats (cocoa butter, coconut oil, coconut butter etc.)

- Small balls or mini muffins size

- Sweet taste

- No sugar, contain only sweeteners – stevia in drops, powder or liquid format, erythritol, xylitol, monk fruit etc.

- Stored in the refrigerator, baked, cooked

- Contain nuts, seeds

- Contain spices such as cinnamon, cardamom, vanilla

- Main ingredients: chocolate, cocoa powder

Kitchen Tools Needed to Prepare the Chocolate Fat Bombs

To prepare the mouthwatering chocolate keto fat bombs fast, you will need to have the right utensils. The following list of kitchen tools will help you prepare your delicious chocolate fat bomb desserts easier and faster.

Food Processor or Blender

Having a food processor or blender is very important for preparing chocolate fat bombs because it will help you to process, grind, pulse, and blend hazelnut spread, chocolate butter, cocoa powder, melted chocolate, coconut butter, or coconut oil.

Electric Hand Mixer

Using an electric hand mixer will save your time and energy, especially when you are preparing chocolate fat bombs where you need to combine various ingredients such as pulsed berries or nuts with cocoa powder or melted chocolate.

Food Scale

The food scale is very important to cook tasty chocolate fat bombs, because you can use it to measure any solid or liquid food, and it will always indicate the quantity of ingredients that you need for preparing the chocolate fat bombs recipes.

Paper Muffin Cups or Candy Cups

Paper muffin cups, candy cups, or silicone molds are crucial when preparing chocolate keto fat bombs, because often you need to bake, to freeze, to store, or to place in the fridge for a long period of time, sometimes even overnight, all your sweet mixtures.

The following chapters contain delicious chocolate keto fat bomb recipes that will sweeten your keto diet days and will have your taste buds come to life!

1. Whole Hazelnuts Chocolate Fat Bombs

Preparation time: 35 minutes

Cooking time: 0 minutes

Servings: 15

Ingredients:

- 8 oz ground hazelnuts
- 10 oz unsweetened dark chocolate
- 8 oz coconut oil
- 25 drops of stevia
- cinnamon
- spray cream

Instructions:

1. Melt the dark chocolate in a double boiler for 20 minutes and mix in the other ingredients.

2. Pour the mixture into the small paper muffin cups or candy cups and place in the fridge for around 4 hours. Serve with the spray cream on top.

Nutrients per serving:

Total Carbs: 2.8g

Net Carbs: 2g

Total Fat: 12g

Protein: 3g

Calories: 78

2. Chocolate and Walnuts Fat Bombs

Preparation time: **25 minutes**

Cooking time: **0 minutes**

Servings: **8**

Ingredients:

- 6 oz unsweetened dark chocolate
- 8 oz coconut oil
- 8 oz cocoa powder
- 4 oz coconut butter
- 15 drops of stevia
- 1 cup walnuts, ground
- vanilla
- sea salt

Instructions:

1. Melt the coconut oil in the microwave and combine it with the cocoa powder, vanilla, stevia, and sea salt.

2. Pour the mixture into the small paper muffin cups or silicone molds and place in the fridge for around 30 minutes.

3. Add half of a teaspoon of coconut butter into each silicone mold or paper muffin cup and spread it with the spatula.

4. Melt the dark chocolate on low heat for around 15 minutes, stirring all the time.

5. Cool the mixture and slowly pour it over the fat bombs, adding ground walnuts on top.

6. The fat bombs should be placed in the fridge for at least 4 hours.

Nutrients per serving:

Total Carbs: 3g

Net Carbs: 2.1g

Total Fat: 15g

Protein: 3.5g

Calories: 88

3. Cocoa and Coconut Fat Bombs

Preparation time: **25 minutes**

Cooking time: **10 minutes**

Servings: **12**

Ingredients:

- 10 oz cocoa powder
- 10 oz shredded coconut
- 7 oz coconut oil
- 7 oz cocoa butter
- 5 oz unsweetened chocolate butter
- 25 drops of stevia
- vanilla

Instructions:

1. Preheat the oven to 330° - 350° Fahrenheit.

2. Toast the coconut for 10 minutes and then pulse using a blender.

3. Add the remaining ingredients except for the spray cream, place into a food processor and blend until smooth.

4. Spoon the mixture into small paper muffin cups or candy cups and place in the fridge for around 4 hours.

Nutrients per serving:

Total Carbs: 2.4g

Net Carbs: 1.5g

Total Fat: 13g

Protein: 3.2g

Calories: 84

4. Orange Taste and Pine Nuts Chocolate Fat Bombs

Preparation time: **25 minutes**

Cooking time: **10 minutes**

Servings: **12**

Ingredients:

- 3 teaspoons orange zest, minced
- 5 oz unsweetened dark chocolate
- 5 oz pine nuts
- 5 oz cottage cheese
- 8 oz cocoa butter
- 5 oz coconut oil
- 10 oz cocoa powder
- 20 drops of stevia
- cinnamon

Instructions:

1. Pulse 5 oz of the pine nuts using a blender.
2. Melt the cocoa butter and dark chocolate in a skillet for 15 minutes, and then add in the cottage cheese.
3. Combine the orange zest, pine nuts, coconut oil, cinnamon, stevia, cocoa powder in a bowl. Add the

mixture to the melted cocoa butter-chocolate-cottage cheese mixture and place in the fridge for 1 hour.

4. Form 12 fat bombs out of the mixture and place in the fridge for around 4 hours.

Nutrients per serving:

Total Carbs: 5.9g

Net Carbs: 4.1g

Total Fat: 19g

Protein: 8g

Calories: 117

5. Chocolate and Cherry Fat Bombs

Preparation time: 25 minutes

Cooking time: 0 minutes

Servings: 10

Ingredients:

- 15 oz unsweetened milk chocolate
- 5 oz unsweetened dark chocolate
- 10 fresh cherries
- 4 oz sugar-free cherry syrup
- 8 oz coconut butter
- 4 oz coconut oil
- 10 oz cocoa powder
- 20 drops of stevia

Instructions:

1. Melt the unsweetened milk chocolate and the unsweetened dark chocolate in a double boiler for 20 minutes.

2. In a bowl, add and mix coconut butter, coconut oil, cherry syrup, cocoa powder, and stevia. Mix the mixture with the melted milk chocolate and dark chocolate, using a hand mixer.

3. Spoon the mixture into each small paper muffin cup, candy cup or silicone candy mold and place in the fridge for around 3 hours, serving with a cherry on top.

Nutrients per serving:

Total Carbs: 3.2g

Net Carbs: 2.2g

Total Fat: 17.8g

Protein: 5.9g

Calories: 99

6. Chocolate Butter Fat Bombs

Preparation time: **20 minutes**

Cooking time: **0 minutes**

Servings: **10**

Ingredients:

- 5 oz cocoa powder
- 10 oz unsalted butter
- 5 oz unsweetened dark chocolate
- 6 oz coconut butter
- 6 oz coconut oil
- 8 tablespoons hulled hemp seeds
- 4 oz heavy cream
- 4 oz shredded coconut
- 25 drops of stevia
- vanilla

Instructions:

1. Place all the ingredients except for the shredded coconut and dark chocolate into a food processor and blend until they have a smooth and creamy consistency.

2. Melt the dark chocolate on a low heat, stirring for around 15 minutes.

3. Form 10 fat bombs out of the mixture and slowly pour the melted chocolate over the fat bombs, rolling the balls in the shredded coconut.

4. Cool and then freeze the chocolate butter fat bombs for 1 hour, and then you are free to serve them.

Nutrients per serving:

Total Carbs: 5.2g

Net Carbs: 2.9g

Total Fat: 21g

Protein: 9g

Calories: 169

7. Chocolate and Strawberries Fat Bombs

Preparation time: *25 minutes*

Cooking time: *0 minutes*

Servings: *20*

Ingredients:

- 10 oz unsweetened dark chocolate
- 10 oz unsweetened milk chocolate
- 5 oz fresh strawberries
- 4 oz coconut oil
- 5 oz unsalted butter
- 2 oz cream cheese
- 1 tablespoon erythritol
- 10 drops of stevia

- vanilla
- sugar-free chocolate spray cream

Instructions:

1. Melt the dark chocolate and the milk chocolate in a double boiler for 20 minutes.

2. In a bowl, add and mix all the ingredients except for the chocolate spray cream, using a hand mixer.

3. Spoon the mixture into each small paper muffin cup or candy cup and place in the fridge for around 3 hours, serving with the chocolate spray cream and the strawberries.

Nutrients per serving:

Total Carbs: 3.2g

Net Carbs: 2.9g

Total Fat: 18g

Protein: 7g

Calories: 95

8. Chocolate Butter and Almonds Fat Bombs

Preparation time: 35 minutes

Cooking time: 0 minutes

Servings: 15

Ingredients:

- 5 oz almonds
- 10 oz unsweetened chocolate butter
- 8 oz unsweetened dark chocolate
- 10 oz cottage cheese
- 5 oz cocoa powder
- 8 oz coconut oil
- 20 drops of stevia
- vanilla
- cardamom

Instructions:

1. Melt the 10 oz of the dark chocolate in the microwave, then melt the chocolate butter in a skillet, and add the cottage cheese.

2. Pulse half of the almonds using a blender and combine them with the coconut oil, vanilla, stevia, cocoa powder, except for the cardamom. Mix the

mixture with the melted chocolate, the melted butter and the cottage cheese mixture and cool for 1 hour.

3. Form 10 fat bombs out of the mixture, press the almond inside each ball and sprinkle cardamom on top.

4. Mixture should be placed in the fridge for around 3 hours.

Nutrients per serving:

Total Carbs: 9g

Net Carbs: 6.7g

Total Fat: 29g

Protein: 14.8g

Calories: 174

9. Chocolate and Raspberries Fat Bombs

Preparation time: 20 minutes

Cooking time: 0 minutes

Servings: 15

Ingredients:

- 6 oz fresh raspberries
- 10 oz unsweetened dark chocolate
- 4 oz cream cheese
- 8 oz coconut butter
- 4 oz unsalted butter
- 20 drops of stevia
- 5 oz cocoa powder
- 1 tablespoon of erythritol

- vanilla

Instructions:

1. Melt the 10 oz of the dark chocolate in the microwave and pulse the fresh raspberries using a blender.

2. Blend the cream cheese, unsalted butter, coconut butter, cocoa powder, stevia, melted chocolate, and vanilla using a food processor.

3. Combine the mixture with the pulsed raspberries in a mixing bowl, mashing with a fork, then place in the fridge for 2 hours.

4. Form 15 chocolate and raspberry fat bombs out of the mixture and serve.

Nutrients per serving:

Total Carbs: 7.5g

Net Carbs: 5g

Total Fat: 22g

Protein: 10.4g

Calories: 160

10. Choco Blueberries and Coconut Fat Bombs

Preparation time: 30 minutes

Cooking time: 0 minutes

Servings: 15

Ingredients:

- 5 oz unsweetened milk chocolate
- 5 oz cocoa powder
- 15 oz fresh or frozen blueberries
- 8 oz coconut oil
- 5 oz coconut butter
- 10 drops of stevia
- 4 tablespoons monk fruit sweetener
- vanilla

Instructions:

1. Defrost the frozen blueberries in the microwave if frozen.

2. Place all the ingredients except for the milk chocolate into a food processor and blend until they have a smooth and creamy consistency, and then freeze for 1 hour.

3. Form 15 fat bombs out of the mixture and melt the chocolate on a low heat, stirring for around 10 minutes.

4. Cool the melted chocolate and slowly pour over the blueberries fat bombs, then freeze the fat bombs for 1 hour and you are free to serve them.

Nutrients per serving:

Total Carbs: 7.9g

Net Carbs: 6g

Total Fat: 18g

Protein: 7.8g

Calories: 110

11. Choco Coconut Fat Bombs

Preparation time: 20 minutes

Cooking time: 0 minutes

Servings: 15

Ingredients:

- 10 oz chocolate butter or hazelnut spread
- 5 oz shredded coconut
- 10 oz cocoa powder
- 6 oz coconut oil
- 4 oz heavy cream
- 20 drops of stevia
- sugar-free chocolate spray cream
- sugar-free chocolate breakfast flakes

Instructions:

1. Place all the ingredients except for the chocolate spray cream into a food processor and blend until they have a smooth and creamy consistency.

2. Spoon the sweet chocolate mixture into the silicone molds or paper muffin cups and freeze for around 3 hours, serving with the chocolate spray cream and chocolate breakfast flakes on top.

Nutrients per serving:

Total Carbs: 4.6g

Net Carbs: 3.2g

Total Fat: 16g

Protein: 5g

Calories: 155

12. Chocolate, Almonds and Coconuts Fat Bombs

Preparation time: 25 minutes

Cooking time: 0 minutes

Servings: 15

Ingredients:

- 10 oz unsweetened milk chocolate
- 5 oz cocoa powder
- 4 oz coconut oil
- 2 oz coconut butter
- 5 oz almonds
- 5 oz cream cheese
- 1 tablespoon of erythritol
- 20 drops of stevia
- 3/4 teaspoon ginger

Instructions:

1. Melt the 10 oz of the milk chocolate in the microwave.
2. Grind half of the almonds and melt the cream cheese adding the coconut oil with the coconut butter.

3. Mix all of your ingredients in a mixing bowl, pour the mixture into the silicone molds and press the almond inside each bomb.

4. Freeze the fat bombs for at least 2 hours and then you are free to serve them.

Nutrients per serving:

Total Carbs: 7.3g

Net Carbs: 3.9g

Total Fat: 18g

Protein: 7g

Calories: 93

13.   Chocolate Berries Fat Bombs

Preparation time: 20 minutes

Cooking time: 0 minutes

Servings: 20

Ingredients:

- 10 oz unsweetened dark chocolate
- 10 oz cocoa powder
- 5 oz mixed berries, frozen
- 5 oz unsweetened chocolate butter
- 10 oz cream cheese
- 20 drops of stevia
- 4 tablespoons monk fruit sweetener
- vanilla

- sugar-free spray cream

Instructions:

1. Defrost the frozen berries mix in the microwave and then melt the 10 oz of the dark chocolate in the microwave.

2. Place all the ingredients except for the spray cream into a food processor and blend until smooth and creamy consistency.

3. Pour the mixture into each small paper muffin cup, candy cup or silicone mold and freeze for overnight, serving with a spray cream on top.

Nutrients per serving:

Total Carbs: 8.7g

Net Carbs: 4.8g

Total Fat: 17g

Protein: 9g

Calories: 102

14.   Choco Hazelnuts and Vanilla Fat Bombs

Preparation time: 25 minutes

Cooking time: 50 minutes

Servings: 10

Ingredients:

- 4 cups of hazelnuts
- 15 oz cocoa powder
- 1 egg
- 1 cup flour
- 8 oz unsweetened chocolate butter
- 2 tablespoons cream cheese
- 25 drops of stevia
- vanilla

Instructions:

1. Preheat the oven to 300°-320°Fahrenheit.
2. Toast the hazelnuts in the oven for 10 minutes and then grind them using a blender.
3. Combine the hazelnuts and all the remaining ingredients in a mixing bowl, using a hand mixer.

4. Make the crumbly dough, spoon the mixture into the silicone molds or candy cups and bake for 50 minutes at 300°- 320°Fahrenheit.

5. Cool the hazelnuts fat bombs for around 2 hours and then you are free to serve them.

Nutrients per serving:

Total Carbs: 6.5g

Net Carbs: 3.6g

Total Fat: 15g

Protein: 7g

Calories: 69

15. Dark and Milk Chocolate with Walnuts Fat Bombs

Preparation time: 25 minutes

Cooking time: 15 minutes

Servings: 14

Ingredients:

- 10 oz unsweetened dark chocolate
- 5 oz unsweetened milk chocolate
- 4 oz cocoa butter
- 4 oz unsweetened chocolate butter
- 4 oz coconut oil
- 25 drops of stevia
- vanilla

- walnut halves

- sugar-free chocolate spray cream

Instructions:

1. Melt together the dark chocolate, the milk chocolate and the cocoa butter in a double boiler for 15 minutes and mix with the other ingredients using a hand mixer.

2. Spoon the mixture into the silicone molds or paper muffin cups and place in the fridge for 4 hours.

3. Remove the fat bombs from the molds and serve with the chocolate spray cream and the walnut halves on top.

Nutrients per serving:

Total Carbs: 4.2g

Net Carbs: 3.5g

Total Fat: 20g

Protein: 7.5g

Calories: 141

16.   Choco Strawberries and Coconut Fat Bombs

Preparation time: 25 minutes

Cooking time: 0 minutes

Servings: 15

Ingredients:

- 8 oz fresh or frozen strawberries
- 8 oz coconut oil
- 5 oz coconut butter
- 5 oz unsweetened chocolate butter
- 4 oz coconut flour
- 10 oz cocoa powder
- 15 drops of stevia
- 4 tablespoons monk fruit sweetener
- vanilla
- sugar-free chocolate spray cream

Instructions:

1. Defrost the frozen strawberries in your microwave if frozen.

2. Place all the ingredients into a food processor and blend until they have a smooth and creamy consistency.

3. Spoon the sweet mixture into the silicone molds or paper muffin cups and freeze for around 3 hours serving with a chocolate spray cream on top.

Nutrients per serving:

Total Carbs: 9.2g

Net Carbs: 6.3g

Total Fat: 17g

Protein: 7g

Calories: 115

17. Chocolate and Coconut Bricks Fat Bombs

Preparation time: 25 minutes

Cooking time: 0 minutes

Servings: 15

Ingredients:

- 10 oz unsweetened dark chocolate
- 8 oz coconut butter
- 4 oz coconut oil
- 5 oz cocoa powder
- 8 oz unsweetened chocolate butter
- 3 tablespoons erythritol
- 10 drops of stevia

- vanilla

- sugar-free chocolate syrup

Instructions:

1. Melt the 10 oz of the dark chocolate in the microwave.

2. Combine the melted dark chocolate with coconut butter, coconut oil, erythritol, cocoa powder, chocolate butter, stevia, and vanilla in a mixing bowl, mashing with a fork until they have a creamy and smooth consistency.

3. Spoon the sweet mixture into silicone pan and spread it with the spatula.

4. Add the chocolate syrup on top and place in the fridge for 4 hours.

Nutrients per serving:

Total Carbs: 7g

Net Carbs: 5g

Total Fat: 17g

Protein: 8.4g

Calories: 139

18.   Spicy Chocolate Fat Bombs

Preparation time: 30 minutes

Cooking time: 0 minutes

Servings: 15

Ingredients:

- 10 oz unsweetened dark chocolate
- 5 oz cocoa powder
- half teaspoon chili pepper
- half teaspoon cayenne pepper
- 8 oz cocoa butter
- 5 oz coconut oil
- vanilla

Instructions:

1. Melt the unsweetened dark chocolate in the microwave.
2. Melt the coconut oil and cocoa butter in a pan over low heat for 15 minutes.
3. Add the chocolate, vanilla, cocoa powder, chili pepper, cayenne pepper and mix all the ingredients.
4. Pour the mixture into 15 small paper muffin cups or candy cups and place in the fridge for around 3 hours.

Nutrients per serving:

Total Carbs: 9.5g

Net Carbs: 6g

Total Fat: 19.8g

Protein: 8g

Calories: 159

19.   Chocolate Pistachio Fat Bombs

Preparation time: 25 minutes

Cooking time: 20 minutes

Servings: 12

Ingredients:

- 8 oz unsweetened white chocolate
- 10 oz cocoa powder
- 8 oz coconut oil
- 4 oz ground pistachio nuts
- 4 oz almond flour
- 4 egg whites
- 15 drops of stevia
- shredded coconut

- vanilla

Instructions:

1. Place the cocoa powder, shredded coconut, almond flour and stevia into a food processor and blend until smooth.

2. Melt the coconut oil in the microwave and combine it with the vanilla and ground pistachio nuts in a mixing bowl, mashing with a fork.

3. Combine the almond flour mixture with the coconut oil and pistachio mixture in a mixing bowl.

4. Whisk the eggs and add them into the sweet almond-coconut oil mixture.

5. Form 12 fat bombs out of the mixture and bake them at 330°- 350° Fahrenheit for 20 minutes, then cool.

6. Melt the white chocolate on a low heat, stirring for around 15 minutes.

7. Cool the melted white chocolate and slowly pour over the fat bombs, then freeze the fat bombs for 1 hour and you are free to serve them.

Nutrients per serving:

Total Carbs: 9.1g

Net Carbs: 6g

Total Fat: 18g

Protein: 10g

Calories: 149

20.   Sesame Seeds Choco Fat Bombs

Preparation time: 25 minutes

Cooking time: 0 minutes

Servings: 12

Ingredients:

- 10 oz sesame seeds
- 4 oz coconut butter
- 4 oz almond butter
- 4 oz coconut oil
- 15 oz cocoa powder
- 15 drops of stevia
- vanilla
- sugar-free chocolate syrup

Instructions:

1. In a pan, toast the sesame seeds for 5 minutes and set aside.
2. Melt the coconut oil, coconut butter and almond butter in the microwave and mix together.
3. Combine the cocoa powder, stevia, sesame seeds and vanilla with the coconut oil mixture in a mixing bowl, mashing with a fork until smooth.

4. Pour the mixture into the small silicone molds and place in the fridge for around 2 hours serving with the chocolate syrup on top.

Nutrients per serving:

Total Carbs: 7.9g

Net Carbs: 4.5g

Total Fat: 18g

Protein: 8g

Calories: 167

21.   Chocolate   Cranberries-strawberries Fat Bombs

Preparation time: 25 minutes

Cooking time: 0 minutes

Servings: 10

Ingredients:

- 4 oz fresh or frozen cranberries
- 4 oz fresh strawberries
- 2 oz strawberries syrup
- 10 oz cocoa powder
- 5 oz unsweetened milk chocolate
- 8 oz creamed coconut milk
- 4 oz unsalted butter

- 5 oz coconut oil
- 15 drops of stevia
- spray cream

Instructions:

1. Combine the creamed coconut milk, unsalted butter and cocoa powder with coconut oil in a mixing bowl, mashing with a fork until smooth.

2. Pulse the stevia, strawberries syrup, cranberries, strawberries, coconut milk and coconut oil mixture using a blender.

3. Pour the mixture into the ice cream maker and process for 1 hour.

4. Spoon the sweet mixture into the small silicone molds or an ice tray and freeze for around 2 hours.

5. Melt the milk chocolate on a low heat, stirring for around 10 minutes, then cool it and slowly pour the melted chocolate over the fat bombs.

6. Freeze for around 1 hour and serve with the spray cream and chocolate slices on top.

Nutrients per serving:

Total Carbs: 7g

Net Carbs: 4g

Total Fat: 19.4g

Protein: 8g

Calories: 182

22.   Chocolate and Peanuts Fat Bombs

Preparation time: 30 minutes

Cooking time: 0 minutes

Servings: 15

Ingredients:

- 10 oz ground peanuts
- 4 oz cocoa powder
- 8 oz cottage cheese
- 4 oz unsalted butter
- 4 oz coconut oil
- 2 oz cream
- 5 oz unsweetened dark chocolate
- 25 drops of stevia
- vanilla
- cardamom

Instructions:

1. Melt the unsalted butter and the cottage cheese in a skillet.
2. Combine the cocoa powder, coconut oil, vanilla, cardamom, stevia, except for the dark chocolate and

ground peanuts. Add the mixture to the melted butter and cottage cheese and cool.

3. Melt the dark chocolate on a low heat, stirring and adding cream for around 10 minutes.

4. Form the fat bombs out of the mixture, slowly pour the melted chocolate over the fat bombs and sprinkle the grated peanuts on top.

5. Sweet peanuts fat bombs should be placed in the fridge for around 3 hours.

Nutrients per serving:

Total Carbs: 5.5g

Net Carbs: 3.1g

Total Fat: 18g

Protein: 6.8g

Calories: 124

23.   Chocolate Nuts Fat Bombs

Preparation time: 25 minutes

Cooking time: 0 minutes

Servings: 20

Ingredients:

- 4 oz ground peanuts
- 4 oz ground walnuts
- 4 oz ground hazelnuts
- 10 oz peanut butter
- 8 oz coconut oil
- 10 oz cocoa powder
- 7 oz coconut flour
- 30 drops of stevia

- sugar-free chocolate spray cream

Instructions:

1. Melt the unsalted butter and coconut oil in a skillet over medium heat.

2. Add all the remaining ingredients except for the chocolate spray cream and melt on a low heat, stirring for around 20 minutes until they have a creamy and smooth consistency.

3. Cool and pour the mixture into each small silicone mold and freeze for 2 hours serving with a chocolate spray cream on top.

Nutrients per serving:

Total Carbs: 6.7g

Net Carbs: 5g

Total Fat: 21g

Protein: 7g

Calories: 184

24.   Vanilla, Strawberries and White Chocolate Fat Bombs

Preparation time: 25 minutes

Cooking time: 0 minutes

Servings: 15

Ingredients:

- 5 oz strawberries
- 8 oz unsweetened white chocolate
- 4 oz cream cheese
- 5 oz unsalted butter
- 4 oz coconut oil
- 20 drops of stevia
- 3 tablespoons monk fruit sweetener
- vanilla

Instructions:

1. Melt 6 oz of the white chocolate in the microwave and pulse the strawberries using a blender.

2. Blend the cream cheese, unsalted butter, coconut oil, stevia, chocolate, monk fruit sweetener and vanilla until smooth using a food processor.

3. Combine the mixture with the pulsed strawberries in a mixing bowl, mashing with a fork, then place in the fridge for 2 hours.

4. Form 15 strawberry fat bombs out of the mixture and serve.

Nutrients per serving:

Total Carbs: 8g

Net Carbs: 5.6g

Total Fat: 15g

Protein: 7g

Calories: 94

25.   Chocolate Lemon Taste Fat Bombs

Preparation time: 30 minutes

Cooking time: 0 minutes

Servings: 16

Ingredients:

- 5 tablespoons lemon zest, minced
- 10 oz unsweetened dark chocolate
- 2 oz unsweetened milk chocolate
- 8 oz coconut butter
- 3 oz coconut oil
- 8 oz cocoa powder
- 20 drops of stevia
- cinnamon

Instructions:

1. Melt the chocolate in the microwave and combine it with the stevia, cinnamon, coconut oil, coconut butter, lemon zest, and cocoa powder.

2. Spoon the mixture into each small paper muffin cup, candy cup or silicone candy mold and place in the fridge for around 3 hours.

Nutrients per serving:

Total Carbs: 4.2g

Net Carbs: 2.5g

Total Fat: 15g

Protein: 7g

Calories: 76

26. Raspberries and Oranges Chocolate Fat Bombs

Preparation time: **15 minutes**

Cooking time: **0 minutes**

Servings: **15**

Ingredients:

- 4 oz fresh raspberries
- 4 tablespoons orange zest, minced
- 5 oz unsweetened dark chocolate
- 5 oz cocoa butter
- 3 oz coconut oil
- 20 drops of stevia
- vanilla
- sugar-free chocolate spray cream

Instructions:

1. Melt 5 oz of the dark chocolate in your microwave.
2. Melt the coconut oil and cocoa butter in a pan over low heat for 15 minutes.
3. Add the vanilla and stevia drops and mix all the ingredients except for the raspberries and chocolate spray cream, using a hand mixer.

4. Fill the paper muffin cups or candy cups with mixture and add the chocolate spray cream with raspberries on top and place in the fridge for around 3 hours.

Nutrients per serving:

Total Carbs: 4.5g

Net Carbs: 3g

Total Fat: 18g

Protein: 6g

Calories: 86

27. Dark Chocolate and Coconuts Fat Bombs

Preparation time: 20 minutes

Cooking time: 25 minutes

Servings: 10

Ingredients:

- 10 oz dark chocolate 95% cocoa
- 10 oz cocoa powder
- 5 oz shredded coconut
- 8 oz cottage cheese or curd
- 4 oz cream cheese
- 8 oz coconut butter
- 5 oz coconut oil

- 15 drops of stevia
- vanilla

Instructions:

1. Melt the coconut oil and coconut butter in a pan over low heat for 15 minutes.

2. Place the cottage cheese, cream cheese, stevia, cocoa powder, coconut oil, shredded coconut and coconut butter into a food processor and blend until they have a smooth and creamy consistency.

3. Form 10 fat bombs out of the mixture and place them in the fridge for 1 hour.

4. Melt the chocolate on a low heat, stirring for around 10 minutes.

5. Cool the mixture and slowly pour it over the fat bombs.

6. The fat bombs should be placed in the fridge for at least 3 hours.

Nutrients per serving:

Total Carbs: 8.7g

Net Carbs: 5.2g

Total Fat: 25g

Protein: 11g

Calories: 98

28.   Walnuts and Berries Chocolate Fat Bombs

Preparation time: 20 minutes

Cooking time: 10 minutes

Servings: 15

Ingredients:

- 5 oz ground walnuts
- 10 oz cocoa powder
- 10 oz unsweetened white chocolate
- 4 oz fresh blackcurrants
- 4 oz fresh strawberries
- 4 oz dreid wild blueberries
- 8 oz coconut butter
- 8 oz coconut oil
- 10 drops of stevia
- 4 tablespoons monk fruit sweetener
- 2 oz cream
- vanilla

Instructions:

1. Place all the ingredients except for the white chocolate and cream into a food processor and

blend until they have a smooth and creamy consistency.

2. Form 10 fat bombs out of the mixture and place them in the fridge for 1 hour.

3. Melt the chocolate on low heat, stirring and adding cream for around 10 minutes.

4. Cool the mixture and slowly pour it over the fat bombs.

5. Freeze the fat bombs for at least 2 hours and then you are free to serve them.

Nutrients per serving:

Total Carbs: 9.1g

Net Carbs: 7g

Total Fat: 19g

Protein: 8g

Calories: 157

29. Gooseberries and Raspberries Choco Fat Bombs

Preparation time: 25 minutes

Cooking time: 0 minutes

Servings: 12

Ingredients:

- 4 oz fresh gooseberries
- 5 oz fresh or frozen raspberries
- 8 oz unsweetened dark chocolate
- 8 oz cottage cheese or curd
- 8 oz coconut butter
- 7 oz coconut oil
- 4 tablespoons monk fruit sweetener

- 15 drops of stevia
- vanilla

Instructions:

1. Place the cottage cheese, stevia, coconut oil, and coconut butter into a food processor and blend until smooth.

2. Pulse the gooseberries and the raspberries using a blender and mix them with the cottage cheese, stevia, coconut oil and coconut butter up to a homogeneous mass.

3. Form 12 fat bombs out of the mixture and place them in the fridge for 1 hour.

4. Melt the chocolate on low heat, stirring for around 10 minutes.

5. Cool the mixture and slowly pour it over the gooseberries fat bombs.

6. Sprinkle the cinnamon on top and place the fat bombs in the fridge for at least 5 hours.

Nutrients per serving:

Total Carbs: 9g

Net Carbs: 7.4g

Total Fat: 18g

Protein: 9g

Calories: 123

30. Macadamia Nuts Chocolate Fat Bombs

Preparation time: 30 minutes

Cooking time: 0 minutes

Servings: 15

Ingredients:

- 8 oz macadamia nuts
- 10 oz cocoa powder
- 5 oz unsalted butter
- 2 oz cream cheese
- 3 oz coconut oil
- 20 drops of stevia
- 3 tablespoons monk fruit sweetener
- vanilla
- walnuts
- sugar-free chocolate spray cream

Instructions:

1. Grind the macadamia nuts and mix with the blended cream cheese and butter using a food processor.

2. Combine the mixture with the other ingredients except for the spray cream, mashing with a fork until smooth, and then place in the fridge for 2 hours.

3. Form 15 macadamia nuts fat bombs out of the mixture and add the walnut halves or the chocolate spray cream on top.

Nutrients per serving:

Total Carbs: 7.7g

Net Carbs: 5g

Total Fat: 14g

Protein: 6.8g

Calories: 69

Conclusion

Thank you for using this cookbook and preparing the chocolate keto fat bombs.

If you are new in the field of sweet and especially chocolate keto fat bombs, this cookbook will help you to start your chocolate keto journey. Hope that you enjoyed the experimenting and preparing these chocolate fat bomb desserts as I did!

If you've enjoyed this book, I'd greatly appreciate if you could leave an honest review on Amazon.

Reviews are very important to us authors, and it only takes a minute for you to post.

Your direct feedback could be used to help other readers to discover the advantages on going keto!

If you have anything you want me to know, any questions, suggestions or feedback, please don't hesitate to contact me.

If you have success story, please send it to me! I'm always happy to hear about my reader's success!

Thank you again and I hope you have enjoyed chocolate keto desserts cookbook.

Other Cookbooks by Brendan Fawn

VEG RECIPES

KETO FAT BOMBS

Keto Fat Bombs: 30 Sweet Fat Bomb Recipes and Keto Desserts

Made in the USA
Monee, IL
10 April 2021

65366455R00048